Carl Linnaeus

GREAT MINDS OF SCIENCE

Carl Linnaeus
Father of Classification

Margaret J. Anderson

Enslow Publishers, Inc.

44 Fadem Road	PO Box 38
Box 699	Aldershot
Springfield, NJ 07081	Hants GU12 6BP
USA	UK

To Norman

Library of Congress Cataloging-in-Publication Data

Anderson, Margaret Jean, 1931–
    Carl Linnaeus: father of classification / Margaret J. Anderson.
      p. cm. — (Great minds of science)
    Includes bibliographical references (p.) and index.
    Summary: Profiles the life of the eighteenth-century Swedish naturalist
whose scientific naming of plants and animals provided an international
language of nature.
    ISBN 0-89490-786-7
    1. Linné, Carl von, 1707–1778—Juvenile literature. 2. Naturalists—
Sweden—Biography—Juvenile literature. [1. Linné, Carl von, 1707–1778.
2. Naturalists.] I. Title. II. Series.
QH44.A63 1997
580'.92
[B]—DC21
                          96-48900
                          CIP
                          AC

Printed in the United States of America

10 9 8 7 6 5 4 3 2 1

Illustration Credits: Margaret J. Anderson, pp. 8, 14, 16, 19, 21, 23,
28, 33, 35, 38, 47, 56, 65, 73, 75, 77, 81, 83, 87, 90, 95, 104, 106;
Stephen J. DeLisle, pp. 11, 37, 49; Library of Congress, pp. 44, 100;
C.Y. Li, pp. 54, 68.

Cover Illustration Credits: Library of Congress, (background);
Visuals Unlimited, (inset).

Contents

Pronunciation of Swedish Names

A word about the Swedish place names: Many of them look hard to pronounce, but they can be sounded out. For example, Stenbrohult is Sten-bro-hult. Some vowels have an accent over them. This changes the sound of the vowel. Here is a short guide to some of the vowel sounds.

å—sounds like "o" in hope. (Umeå is pronounced Um-e-oh.)

ö—is pronounced by saying "ah" with rounded lips (Öland is pronounced oe-land.)

ä—sounds like "e" in bet. Växjö is a hard name to say. It is pronounced vek-yhoe.

A New Twig on the Family Tree

STENBROHULT IS A QUIET VILLAGE IN THE south of Sweden. Back in 1704, the church pastor needed an assistant. Nils Linnaeus was chosen for the job. The young man stayed with the pastor's family. He promptly fell in love with Christina, the fifteen-year-old daughter.

Nils and Christina were married two years later. Nils built a simple, turf-roofed house in nearby Råshult for his bride. Next to their new home, he planted an unusual border. The shrubs were arranged like guests around a dinner table covered with flowers. Many of the plants were

Nils Linnaeus built this turf-roofed house for his bride Christina, in Råshult, Sweden. This house became the birthplace of Carl Linnaeus.

not known in Sweden. Nils's uncle had brought them from Germany.

On May 23, 1707, a son was born to Christina and Nils Linnaeus. They named him Carl. Carl Linnaeus grew up to be the most famous botanist of all time. Perhaps his father's interest in flowers gave him a head start. Nils used to decorate the baby's cradle with blossoms. As Carl grew older, Nils often gave him flowers to play with.

In 1708, the year after Carl was born, Christina's father died. Nils became senior pastor, and the family moved back to Christina's old home next to the church. Later, Carl described the setting as "one of the most beautiful places in all Sweden, for it lies on the big lake of Möckeln. . . . [It] is surrounded on all sides by flat tilled land, except to the west where it is lapped by the clear waters of the lake. Away to the south are lovely beech woods, to the north the high mountain ridge of Taxås. . . ."[1]

One sunny afternoon, when Carl was about four, the Linnaeus family and some friends went on a picnic by the lake. They gathered bunches of wildflowers. Nils told his guests what each flower was called. After that, Carl wanted to know the name of every plant in the garden and nearby fields. These names were long strings of words in Latin. The little boy had a hard time remembering them. He asked his father to repeat them again and again. Nils told the child sharply that he was not going to tell him names just to have them forgotten. From that day on, Carl gave his whole mind to learning them. Names became his passion.

By the time Carl Linnaeus was a university student, he knew all the flowers in his home province. He traveled to the reindeer country of Lapland in the far north looking for new plants. He was also interested in the birds, mammals, and insects. He collected fossils and rocks. Carl Linnaeus became an important naturalist, but what earned him his place among the great scientists of the world was his love of names and his orderly mind. Linnaeus put all his effort into arranging and classifying his finds.

Carl Linnaeus's talents met a great need. The eighteenth century was a time of widening horizons. Many European settlers were moving to the New World. North America was rich in strange, unknown plants and animals. Explorers brought specimens from other distant lands. Eighteenth-century scientists believed in a well-ordered universe. Naming new plants and animals was an important first step.

Linnaeus was not satisfied with the system of naming used at that time. He decided to reform it. This was a huge job. It "demanded time and

When Linnaeus was born, Sweden was one of the most powerful nations in Europe. After several disastrous wars against Russia, however, Sweden lost most of its influence.

almost did away with sleep."[2] He gave each kind of plant or animal just two names. The first told the genus (group) to which the plant or animal belonged. The second name described the species within that group. This two-word system of naming is known as the binomial system of nomenclature.

Linnaeus's names were logical and easy to learn. Maybe he adopted a two-word system because he had had a hard time remembering the long names of flowers when he was a small boy. The binomial system had actually been tried a hundred years earlier by Gaspard Bauhin, a Swiss doctor and botanist. In 1623, he wrote a book naming and describing the six thousand kinds of known plants.

A two-word system is also used in naming some everyday objects. For example, we speak of carving knives, dinner knives, steak knives, pocket knives, and hunting knives. These are all different kinds of knives. The first part of each knife's name tells us which type of knife it is. Linnaeus's system worked the same way, but he wrote in Latin because that was the language of science. In Latin, the noun is placed before the adjective, so the group name comes first. Related types of plants or animals share the same *first* name. The *second* word is an adjective that describes a special characteristic.

Let's take a closer look at an example of binomial naming. Linnaeus called white clover *Trifolium repens*. *Trifolium* means "three leaves," which comes from the typical clover shape of the plant's leaves. *Repens* means "creeping." The stems creep close to the ground. Crimson clover is called *Trifolium incarnatum*. *Incarnatum* means "blood red." White and crimson clover share the same first name. They are both kinds of clover. They belong to the same genus. In botany books, the names are followed by the letter *L*. That tells us that Linnaeus named them.

Although Latin is no longer spoken, giving plants and animals Latin names has worked out well. It means that the scientific name is the same in every language. Common names often vary from place to place, even where the same

Shown here is a statue of Linnaeus with a linden tree supporting his bust. The Linnaeus family took their name from the Swedish word linn, for the linden tree.

language is spoken. Linnaeus's own name is a good example.[3] It comes from the Swedish word *linn*, which means "linden tree." In Britain, the linden is known as the lime tree, although it has nothing to do with the tree that grows the lime fruit. In some parts of North America, the linden is called basswood; in other places it is the whitewood tree. However, the tree's Latin name, *Tilia*, is the same everywhere.

If Linnaeus wanted to name a plant using a word that did not occur in Latin, he simply added a Latin ending. For example, Linnaeus called the tobacco plant *Nicotiana tabacum*. He named the genus *Nicotiana* after Jean Nicot, who introduced tobacco growing into France. The species name is from a Native American name for the tobacco plant.

The study of naming and classifying plants and animals is called taxonomy. Two other seventeenth-century taxonomists laid the foundation for Linnaeus's important work. One was John Ray, an Englishman. He based his system of classifying plants on several features—fruits, flowers, and leaves. Joseph Tournefort, a French botanist, looked only at the shape of the petals. Linnaeus divided plants into different classes based on the number and position of the stamens. His was an easier system to describe and to use.

Linnaeus named so many plants and animals that he has been called "God's Registrar."[4] The number of times *L.* appears after a scientific name shows how hard he worked at naming

This drawing is of **Linnea borealis,** *which is the only plant that is named after Linnaeus. The common name for this plant is twinflower.*

things. He often honored his friends by naming plants after them. However, only one flower bears his name. *Linnea borealis*, the twinflower, was his favorite plant. He loved to see its delicate pink blossoms on the forest floor in early summer.

2

School Days

CHRISTINA LINNAEA WANTED CARL TO be a pastor like his father and his grandfather before him. When he was seven, his parents hired a tutor. Carl did not get along with him. He did not like to study. He would much rather be out in the garden than indoors reading. His mother nagged, but his father usually took his side. In his autobiography, Carl later described his father as being "very gentle, calm, and kindly." His mother, on the other hand, was "shrewd, lively, and diligent."[1]

When Carl was nine, Nils finally agreed that the boy needed to study harder. He was sent off to school in Växjö, a country town about thirty miles away. Carl found it hard to say good-bye to the lake, the fields, and the garden that he loved. It was also hard to leave his parents and his three younger sisters. The following year, a little brother was born.

The teachers in Växjö did not turn Carl into

After the death of his father-in-law, Nils Linnaeus took over as pastor at Stenbrohult Church. Nils hoped that his son Carl would eventually succeed him as pastor as well.

a scholar, either. Schooldays were long and boring. Classes began at 6 A.M. and lasted until 5 P.M. Most of that time was spent learning Latin and Greek, or studying the Bible. The teachers were so severe that they made the students' "hair stand on end."[2]

Carl was still interested in plants. He spent his holidays exploring the countryside. Sometimes he went off looking for flowers instead of attending class. Although he had plenty of friends, he liked to be alone. The other students nicknamed him "the little botanist."[3]

Even in high school, Carl thought that most classes were a waste of time. Greek and Hebrew were taught because many students wanted to be pastors. Carl did like logic and physics, however. They were taught by Johan Rothman, the town doctor. Dr. Rothman took a liking to Carl. He showed him that botany could be a serious study. He encouraged him and lent him books.

Toward the end of Carl's school years, his father visited Växjö. He was concerned about his health and had decided to consult Dr. Rothman.[4] While he was in town, he asked Carl's

Nils Linnaeus (shown here) was upset when he learned that Carl was not suited to be a pastor. However, Dr. Rothman felt that Carl would be better off if he tried to further his interest in plants.

teachers how his son was doing in school. Their answer must have come as a shock. They told Nils Linnaeus that his son was a hopeless student. He had no chance of becoming a pastor. He would be better off learning a trade. He might be a good shoemaker, but he would never be a clergyman.

Poor Nils! All the money he had spent on Carl's education was wasted! How was he going to break the news to his wife? Feeling very glum, he went to see Dr. Rothman. After they had talked about his health, Nils Linnaeus asked the doctor's advice on what to do about Carl. This time the answer was more encouraging. Rothman agreed with the other teachers that Carl would never be a clergyman, but he did not think he should be a shoemaker. He thought that Carl should be a doctor. Carl's keen interest in plants would carry him a long way. Medical students needed a thorough knowledge of botany. At that time, almost all medicines were made from native plants.

Nils Linnaeus was not completely won over.

Christina Linnaea is pictured here in her wedding gown. She, too, was not pleased when she learned that Carl would not become a pastor as she had hoped.

Christina would be unhappy that their plans for Carl's career were not working out. A pastor's job was more secure than a doctor's. Should they be spending still more money on Carl's education when there were the younger children to worry about?

Dr. Rothman came up with a generous offer. He said that Carl could live with him for the next year. Carl would be his private student until he was ready to go to the university.

The plan worked out well. The doctor taught Carl some anatomy and physiology. He also introduced him to Tournefort's method of classifying plants by the shape of their petals. At the end of the school year, when Carl returned to Stenbrohult, he spent the long summer days studying flowers. He worked on his plant collection. He followed Tournefort's method of classification. Sometimes it worked. Sometimes it did not.

Lund University

CARL LINNAEUS SET OUT FOR LUND University in August 1727. He chose Lund because that was where his father had studied. Also, a family friend held the high post of Dean of the Cathedral. As Carl rode into town, all the bells were tolling. When he asked someone why, he learned that the dean had just died. Things were off to a poor start.

Linnaeus did not like what he could see of Lund. Geese and pigs wandered up and down the dirty streets rooting through the filth and garbage. The university itself was no more promising than the town. Only one professor lectured in medicine. No one taught botany.

Linnaeus rented a room from Lund's leading doctor. Dr. Stobaeus was interested in natural history. He had his own museum of birds, plants, rocks, and shells. He also had a large herbarium (collection of dried plants) and a good library.

Dr. Stobaeus was a short-tempered man. Maybe this was because he suffered from headaches, was lame, and was blind in one eye. He was also a very busy man. One day, while his secretary was out, he asked Linnaeus to answer some letters. Linnaeus did such a poor job that the letters could not be sent. He had lost a chance to make a good impression on the famous doctor.

Lund is close to the sea. To escape from the dirty town, Linnaeus often went out into the countryside looking for plants. He explored the flat salt marshes and meadows. He found plants that did not grow in the rolling hills around Stenbrohult. He noted that different types of plants belong in different types of surroundings.

He was anxious to know the names of these unfamiliar plants. The books in the doctor's library would surely provide answers, but the library was always kept locked.

The doctor's secretary, who was also a student, had a key to the library. He and Linnaeus were good friends. The secretary agreed to sneak books out of the library for Linnaeus. In return, Linnaeus promised to help him with his physiology homework.

Night after night, Linnaeus stayed up late, poring over the borrowed books by candlelight. The doctor's old mother slept in a nearby room. She saw the light shining in Carl's room late at night. She thought that the careless young man had fallen asleep with a candle still burning. The house was old and was built of wood. An open flame could easily start a fire. One evening she spoke to the doctor about her fears.

At two o'clock the following morning, Dr. Stobaeus burst into Linnaeus's room. He expected to find Linnaeus sleeping. Instead, he was sitting at a table surrounded by a pile of books.

After high school, Linnaeus continued his education at Lund University. Often, he could be found up late at night reading books from Dr. Stobaeus's library.

When the doctor realized that they were *his* own books from his locked library, he was furious. He demanded an explanation. He listened to what Linnaeus had to say. Then he ordered him to put out the light and go to bed. They would talk again in the morning.

The next day, the interview went far better than Linnaeus had dared to hope. The doctor questioned him about his interest in botany. When he found out how serious Linnaeus was about studying plants, he calmed down. He gave Linnaeus the run of the library. He offered him a free room and meals.

Near the end of the school year, Linnaeus was bitten on the arm while he was looking for plants. The arm puffed up. Blood poisoning set in, and Dr. Stobaeus became alarmed. He called in a surgeon, who cut the arm from the elbow to the armpit to let the poison out. After Linnaeus recovered, he gave a lot of thought to the creature that had caused him so much trouble. He decided (probably wrongly) that he had been attacked by a small worm. Later, he got revenge on the worm by naming it *Furia infernalis*. This means "a fury from hell"!

Linnaeus went home to Stenbrohult for the summer. One day, Dr. Rothman came over to visit. When he heard that botany was not taught at Lund, he advised Carl to transfer to Uppsala University. Uppsala was four hundred miles away. Nils Linnaeus agreed to the change, but when he gave his son money for the journey, he said that this was all the financial help Carl would get from his parents. From then on, he would have to make his own way. Money troubles followed Linnaeus for years.

A Student at Uppsala

UPPSALA STOOD ON THE WEST BANK OF
the Fyris River. A huge castle and a red-brick
cathedral dominated the city. The university had
been founded in 1477. It was the oldest in
Sweden. Today it is a leading university, but in
1728, when Linnaeus enrolled, it was going
through bad times. Although there were twice as
many professors of medicine as at Lund, that
only made two! Both of them were old men.
Their names were Lars Roberg and Olaf
Rudbeck. Rudbeck was in charge of anatomy,
botany, and zoology. He left all his teaching to

his assistant, Nils Rosén. However, Rosén was in Holland getting his degree.

Linnaeus could not find a job, and he soon ran out of money. In his autobiography, he wrote that "he had to borrow to buy food and could not even pay to have his shoes soled, being obliged to lay paper in them. . . . He would gladly have returned to Stobaeus who had treated him so kindly, but he could not afford the journey. Besides, Dr. Stobaeus would have been extremely angry to meet again the youth for whom he had taken such a fancy and who had deserted him without even asking advice."[1]

The following spring, life took a turn for the better. Linnaeus made two friends. One was Peter Artedi, a keen naturalist. Ever since Linnaeus had arrived, he had been hearing about Artedi, who was at home because his father was ill. When Artedi returned to Uppsala in March, Linnaeus finally met him.

The two young men immediately liked one another. They had a lot in common. Both were pastors' sons. Both had disappointed their

After leaving Lund University, Linnaeus arrived at Uppsala University in 1728. This is the Medical Building at Uppsala.

families by not wanting to be pastors themselves. Above all else, they both loved natural history. They were, however, very different in looks and personality. Artedi was tall and solemn. Linnaeus was short, sturdy, and cheerful.

Linnaeus and Artedi wanted to study the entire plant and animal kingdoms. This was such a big undertaking that they decided to divide the work between them. Artedi took the amphibians, reptiles, and fish. Linnaeus took the birds and insects. He also got most of the plants, except for the parsley family. Artedi was working on a way to arrange or classify this family. Linnaeus decided he would organize the rest of the plant kingdom.

Linnaeus and Artedi agreed on one more point. If one of them should die, the other would make sure that any unfinished work was published. This sad task fell to Linnaeus only eight years later.

The other friend that Linnaeus made that year was Dr. Olaf Celsius. One day, an elderly man asked Linnaeus the names of some plants in the University Botanic Garden. He was impressed by Linnaeus's answers. When he learned that Linnaeus had a collection of more than six hundred kinds of wildflowers, he was even more impressed. He invited Linnaeus to come home with him. Linnaeus then discovered that he had been talking to one of the most important men in Uppsala. Dr. Celsius was a

One day while walking in the University Botanic Garden, Dr. Olaf Celsius asked Linnaeus the names of some plants, and was very impressed with his answer. Today, a statue of Linnaeus stands in that very garden.

Professor of Theology and Dean of the Cathedral.

Dr. Celsius took a liking to young Linnaeus. He not only granted him the use of his library, but he offered him a place to stay. Linnaeus was glad to accept. This solved his money problem. To repay the doctor's kindness, Linnaeus helped him with a book he was writing on all the plants named in the Bible.

At that time, students often would write a poem, as a New Year's present, to honor their favorite professor. Linnaeus wanted to write a poem for Dr. Celsius, but he was not much of a poet. Instead, he gave the doctor a scientific paper he had just written. It was about pollination in plants and explained the role of the stamens and pistil in the formation of seeds.

Celsius was delighted with Linnaeus's paper. He showed it to Professor Rudbeck, who was very impressed. Soon after this, Linnaeus applied to Rudbeck for a post as gardener at the Botanic Gardens. He was disappointed when he did not get the job. Rudbeck, however, had

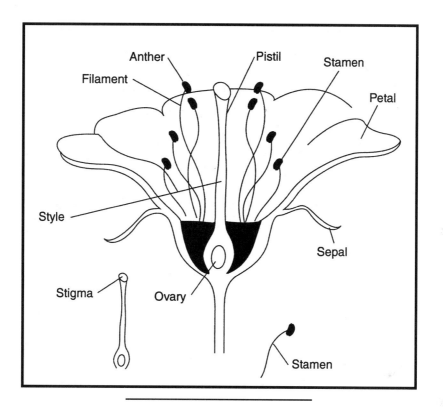

The parts of a flower. Linnaeus classified plants by the number of stamens in their flowers.

something better in mind. He asked Linnaeus to teach botany. Although Linnaeus was only a second-year student, his lectures drew large crowds. Three or four hundred people showed up instead of the usual seventy or eighty students.

Rudbeck was delighted with his new assistant's success. He invited Linnaeus to move into

This house is Professor Rudbeck's house where Carl lived while tutoring Rudbeck's youngest sons. Linnaeus later lived here with his own family.

his home and teach his three youngest sons. The boys were part of a very large family. Rudbeck had been married three times and had twenty-four children!

Later, Linnaeus thanked Rudbeck for all his kindness by naming a plant *Rudbeckia* in his honor. Linnaeus gave a lot of thought as to which to choose. He finally settled on an American plant, the coneflower, which is related to the black-eyed Susan. Linnaeus told Rudbeck that he had chosen the coneflower because it is "a noble plant in order to recall your merits . . . a tall one to give an idea of your stature. . . . Its rayed flowers will bear witness that you shone among [the wise] like the sun among the stars."[2] Rudbeck was, of course, very pleased.

Although he held two jobs, Linnaeus found time for his own work. The fact that so many plants did not fit into the popular methods of classification troubled him. He began to develop a new system. He grouped flowers into twenty-four classes based on the number and position of their stamens. He divided the classes into orders based on the pistils. The orders were divided into genera (the plural of *genus*) by the form of the fruit. Linnaeus was only twenty-three, but he had taken a giant step toward reorganizing the entire plant kingdom.

During the long winter evenings, Rudbeck often told Linnaeus stories of his adventures. As a young man, the professor had traveled to Lapland. He made drawings and notes of the many unusual things he saw. He collected flowers and brought back animal skins and bones. Unfortunately, all his work was lost in a terrible fire that raged through Uppsala in 1702. He encouraged Linnaeus to undertake a similar journey. Linnaeus wanted to go, but the trip would be expensive.

Everything was going well for Linnaeus. His lectures were popular, and his research was exciting. However, this happy state did not last. In March 1731, Rudbeck's assistant, Nils Rosén, returned from Holland with a degree in medicine. He quickly became the most popular doctor in Uppsala. He took over the teaching of anatomy at the university. He also wanted to teach botany, although he knew less about plants than Linnaeus did. Rudbeck decided that Linnaeus could keep his job because he was the better botanist. Rosén was annoyed. His attitude upset Linnaeus, who did not like to be the "the object of jealousy."[3]

Several months later, Linnaeus and Rudbeck's wife had a disagreement. She no longer wanted him to teach the children. Dr. Rudbeck was not brought into the quarrel, but Linnaeus was forced to find somewhere else to live. To add to his troubles, he learned that his mother was seriously ill.

At Christmastime, Linnaeus decided he needed a vacation. He went home to Stenbrohult. Before leaving Uppsala, he applied to the Royal Society of Sciences at Uppsala for a grant to go plant hunting in Lapland. If he got the money, he would have a reason to stay away from Uppsala for some time.

Lapland Adventure

BACK IN THE EIGHTEENTH CENTURY, Lapland was a wild and rugged place. It still is. The people's lifestyle has hardly changed in the last three hundred years. The Lapps follow the migrations of the reindeer herds through the north of Sweden, Norway, and Finland. Lapland is not one country.

Christina Linnaea did not like the idea of her son's going off to such a remote area on his own. Carl told her that he wanted to find new plants and animals. He hoped to discover valuable minerals. Also, he was curious about the customs of the native people. These reasons were not enough for Christina. She kept hoping that the Society would not fund the trip.

Nils Linnaeus was more supportive. He said to Carl, "If you are confident that this journey will advance your career, then ask God for guidance and help."[1] As it turned out, the journey did make a big difference to his son's future.

In April, Linnaeus heard that he had been awarded a grant. It was less than he had asked for, but he did not think twice about accepting. He spent the next month getting ready for his big adventure. He would be traveling by horse and on foot. Lightweight gear makes a trip into the wilderness much easier now than it was in those days. In his leather bag, Linnaeus packed an extra shirt, nightcaps, a comb, an inkhorn, a pencase, and a magnifying glass. He took along a gauze veil to keep off insects, his journal, his manuscripts on birds and plants, and lots of sheets of paper for pressing plants.

He set off in high spirits on May 22, 1732, the day before his twenty-fifth birthday. He wore a wool coat, leather breeches, a green cap, and

In the spring of 1732, Linnaeus journeyed north to study the plants and animals of Lapland. Linnaeus is pictured here in Lappish native dress.

his wig. His sword hung by his side. As he headed north, everything he saw delighted him. He often got down from his horse to pick a flower or to examine a rock. He was "like a wide-eyed child among new toys."[2] It took him eleven days to reach his first goal, the northern city of Umeå.

From Umeå, Linnaeus headed west toward Lycksele. It was raining hard. His horse picked its way along the narrow stony track. Toward the evening, he came upon a group of women who were shredding aspen bark to feed to their cows and goats. When he asked if they could provide him with supper, they offered him a woodcock. It had been shot, dried, and salted the previous year. To his surprise, it was quite tasty! That night he slept between reindeer skins and laid his head on a pillow stuffed with reindeer hair.

The next day, he was on the trail early. He had to watch for low branches and clamber over fallen trees. He risked his neck each time he and his stumbling horse crossed a rickety bridge over another swollen stream. In spite of bad roads and miserable weather, Linnaeus did not miss even the smallest plants. Everything was recorded in his journal. He was especially interested in mosses and lichens. Lichens, which form the main part of the reindeer diet, grow in great abundance in the north.

When the roads became impassable, Linnaeus hired a guide and continued the journey by boat. At first, the river was smooth, but then they came to a series of rapids. Linnaeus describes what happened next: "The peasant handed me my things, put his bag of food on his back and, turning round to the boat, laid both oars over it crosswise so that each came under the opposite arm [and then put the boat over his head]. And thus he leaped with them over hill and dale, so fast that the devil himself could hardly have kept up with him."[3]

When they reached Lycksele, Linnaeus called on the pastor and his wife. They wanted him to stay for a few days so that they could let the Lapps know that Linnaeus was coming, because the Lapps did not always welcome strangers.

One of the things that interested Linnaeus the most during his trip to Lapland was lichens. Lichens form the main part of a reindeer's diet.

The next day, however, was warm. The river was rising due to melting snow. If Linnaeus and his guide delayed, travel would not be possible.

They were on the river all that day. They continued through the night. Because they were so far north, it was always "light as day, the sun disappearing below the horizon for only about an hour and a half."[4] The few people they met were too busy fishing to stop and give them food. The guide went ahead in search of help. When he came back, Linnaeus could not tell if the wild-looking creature who accompanied him was a man or a woman. She turned out to be a woman with a great tangle of black hair. Linnaeus was quite afraid of this "Fury" (as he called her in his journal). He asked her for food, and she offered him several fish. This is how Linnaeus described the scene: "I looked at the raw fish, whose mouths were full of worms, and the sight took away my appetite. . . . I asked if I could get reindeer tongues, which the Lapps dry and sell . . . but she said it was not possible. 'Then reindeer cheese?' 'Yes, but it is nearly six miles away.' 'If you have any, could I buy one or two?' She replied, 'I would not want you to die of hunger in my country.'"[5]

After buying a small cheese, Linnaeus retraced his steps to Lycksele. He then returned to Umeå. He was soon ready to continue his journey, this time heading north. His journal entry for June 15, 1732, provides a picture of

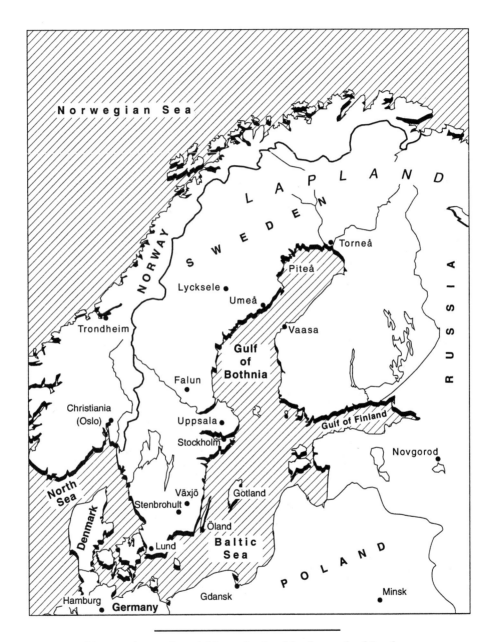

Linnaeus's travels took him to Lapland in the north of Sweden.

some of the discomforts and dangers of this stage of the journey. A cloud of gnats "seemed to occupy the whole atmosphere, especially when I traveled through damp meadows. They filled my mouth, nose and eyes. Luckily they did not bite or sting, though they almost choked me.

"Just at sunset I reached the town of Old Piteå. Near the landing spot stood a gibbet with a couple of wheels on which lay the bodies of two Finlanders without heads. These men had been executed for highway robbery and murder."[6]

Soon after this, Linnaeus came upon some pearl fishermen. They were pulling mussels out of the river with long tongs. To find one pearl, they had to open several thousand mussels. This chance meeting turned out to be important to Linnaeus later on. He figured that the pearl was caused by something being wrong inside the mussel. Thinking about this, he wrote, "Anyone who could induce this illness in mussels could make them produce pearls; if one could, what could be more profitable?"[7]

His route then took him up into the Lapland

Alps, where he shared a crowded hut with sixteen Lapps. Linnaeus did not think much of their table manners. They cleaned their bowls and spoons by spitting on them. Then they wiped them dry with their fingers. In the end, however, he respected the Lapps in spite of their manners.

Linnaeus wanted to travel to the coast of Norway. A seventy-year-old man and another, who was about fifty, offered to show him the way. By the time the three of them reached the coast, Linnaeus was exhausted. The Lapps were still full of energy, even though they had carried all the gear. Linnaeus wondered what made them so healthy. He decided that the pure air and water must be partly responsible. The Lapp outlook and lifestyle also promoted good health. They were not jealous people. They did not quarrel much. They were moderate in their eating and drinking. Later in his career, Linnaeus gave lectures on health and diet. His ideas were ahead of his time, and many are accepted to this day.

On the trip home, Linnaeus followed the coast of the Gulf of Bothnia down into Finland. He met some farmers who told him about a strange illness that affected the cattle each year. Linnaeus solved the problem of the mystery illness. The cattle were eating water hemlock, a poisonous plant. He told the farmers to dig up all the hemlock, and their cattle would be healthy.

On the last day of September, he caught the ferry across the gulf to Sweden. He had been traveling for over four months and had covered more than three thousand miles. He couldn't wait to get back to Uppsala and arrange all his finds.

Back in Uppsala

THE LAPLAND JOURNEY HAD BEEN LONGER and more costly than Linnaeus had planned. He asked the Royal Society of Sciences to make up the difference. Once again, they did not give him as much as he asked for. He was disappointed when only a small part of his report was published in the Society journal. However, he had too much to do to dwell on these setbacks.

When Linnaeus unpacked his specimens, his room began to look like a museum. His bookcase took up one wall, and his Lapp costume was displayed on another. He had thousands of kinds of

After his return from Lapland, Carl Linnaeus began work on his book Flora Lapponica. *When translated into English, the title is* Flowers of Lapland.

insects, as well as boxes and boxes of shells and stones. Pots of rare plants covered the tables. His herbarium included more than three thousand species of pressed flowers. In one corner, thirty different kinds of tame birds perched on the branches of a tree!

Linnaeus and Nils Rosén were still at odds

with one another. Rosén was annoyed that Linnaeus did not attend his anatomy classes. Linnaeus was too busy teaching botany and writing a book on the flowers of Lapland. The fact that his botany lectures were more popular than ever did not help matters.

At Christmas, Linnaeus went home to Stenbrohult. He enjoyed telling his family about his adventures in Lapland. His mother's health was failing. When Linnaeus left for Uppsala, he was afraid that he would not see her again. His fears turned out to be true. Christina Linnaea died the next summer, in 1733.

Linnaeus spent the following Christmas in Falun, in the province of Dalarna. Claes Sohlberg, a fellow student, had invited him to visit his family. After working such long hours in Uppsala, Linnaeus threw himself into the social life. At one party, he met the governor of Dalarna.

Sohlberg's father was an inspector of the mines. He asked Linnaeus if he would like to go down a copper mine. This turned out to be the

Students at Uppsala University watched dissections in the anatomy theater. Although Linnaeus was a medical student, he was too busy teaching classes to attend anatomy lectures.

high point—or the low point—of his stay in Falun. He compared it to visiting hell. After climbing down swaying ladders, he crawled through places so narrow that he had to turn sideways to get through. The miners carried torches in their mouths. He wrote, "There is a constant risk of sudden death from the collapse of a roof, so that they can never feel safe for a single second. The great depth, the dark and the danger, made my hair stand on end with fright, and I wished for one thing only—to be back again on the surface."[1]

Linnaeus returned to Uppsala with more boxes of rocks and minerals. He was happy to have another collection to arrange. He started to write a book on a system for classifying minerals.

By now, Linnaeus had been a student for seven years. His goal was to be a professor of botany. For that, he needed a degree in medicine from a foreign university. Holland was his first choice. It was a gathering place for the scholars of Europe. It was also an important center of printing. He might be able to get his manuscripts published there. He tried to think of some way to pay for the journey.

A letter from the governor of Dalarna saved Linnaeus from having to deal with the problem right then. The governor wanted him to make a complete study of the natural history of Dalarna. Linnaeus was delighted to do so.

This time he did not travel alone. He was now a well-known explorer. Lots of students were eager to go along, paying their own way. Linnaeus settled on seven young men, including his friend Claes Sohlberg. Each student had a different job. One looked after the horses. Another arranged for places to stay along the route. Sometimes they slept in barns; sometimes they boarded with the village pastor. Other students recorded the samples of plants, animals, and minerals. Someone took notes on the way of life of the people they met on their travels.

The governor was so pleased with the report that he invited Linnaeus to stay on at Falun and teach his sons. The job would leave Linnaeus plenty of time for his own writing and studying.

Later in the year, Claes Sohlberg's father offered to pay Linnaeus to travel to Holland with his son. Linnaeus was to help Claes with his studies. Linnaeus quickly accepted. He could complete his degree. He was also keen to visit the famous Botanical Gardens in Amsterdam. Many of the plants were from the New World.

It was now Christmas again. Linnaeus took another well-earned break from his work. At a party, he met a young woman named Sara Lisa Moraea. She was eighteen years old. Linnaeus was twenty-seven. They promptly fell in love.

Sara Lisa's father was the leading doctor in Falun. He did not like the idea of his daughter marrying a poor botanist. Sara Lisa begged, and her father finally gave in. He agreed that she and Carl could become engaged. They had to wait for three years before they married, however. Linnaeus was to go to Holland with Claes Sohlberg as planned. Dr. Moraeus probably thought that a lot could happen in three years.

Clifford's Garden

LINNAEUS AND SOHLBERG SET OUT FOR Holland in April 1735. They traveled through Germany, stopping in Hamburg. People there had heard about Linnaeus's journey to Lapland. They were eager to meet the famous young botanist. Linnaeus enjoyed being a celebrity. He was introduced to the mayor. The mayor showed him a stuffed seven-headed dragon that he was planning to sell for a huge price. Linnaeus quickly pointed out that the dragon was a fake. Its scaly body was made from snakeskins glued together. The heads were from seven weasels.

The mayor was not happy to hear this. Linnaeus and Sohlberg had to leave Hamburg in a hurry.

When they reached Holland, Linnaeus wasted no time in getting his medical degree. He handed in a thesis that he had written in Sweden. It was on the cause of malaria. Although Linnaeus did not know that malaria was passed to people by mosquitoes, he was on the right track. He had noticed that the sickness was common in people living in houses on clay soils. Clay was used as a building material. When houses were built, the clay was dug from pits right next to them. The water that collected in these pits provided a breeding place for mosquitoes.

The next step in getting his degree was an oral exam. After that, Linnaeus diagnosed a case of jaundice. Then he defended his thesis in a public debate. He had earned his degree in less than two weeks! Of course, he had already spent seven years as a university student in Sweden.

Sohlberg's father did not come through with the money he had promised Linnaeus. The two young men drifted apart. Now that he was a doctor, Linnaeus could return to Sweden and to Sara Lisa Moraea. But first, he wanted to meet some of the leading scientists in Holland.

One of the first scientists that Linnaeus got to know was Dr. Johan Gronovius, an important botanist. Linnaeus showed him a manuscript describing his new system for classifying plants. Gronovius was so impressed that he offered to help pay for the cost of having it printed. *Systema Naturae* (A System of Nature) was published in 1735.

In *Systema Naturae*, Linnaeus gave botanists a set of working rules for classifying plants. He divided nature into three kingdoms. He used these characteristics: "Stones grow; plants grow and live; animals grow, live, and feel."[1] The plant kingdom was divided into twenty-four classes, according to the number and position of the stamens. The classes were divided into orders, and the orders into genera.

Although Linnaeus's system greatly advanced the study of botany, it is no longer used. Some plants that are not closely related ended up in the same group. Linnaeus lived a hundred years before Charles Darwin wrote *The Origin Of Species*. Darwin's theory of evolution explained how species can change over time. This gave botanists a clearer understanding of plant relationships. They could then develop a more logical system of classification.

The first edition of *Systema Naturae* was a short book. However, a lot of information was packed into its fourteen large pages. Linnaeus revised *Systema Naturae* many times over the next thirty years. In later editions, he adopted the binomial system of nomenclature. The twelfth edition, completed in 1768, ran to three volumes and 2,300 pages.

To stay longer in Holland, Linnaeus needed to find a way to support himself. His problem was solved when Dr. Johannes Burman invited him to be his guest. In return, he was to help Burman with a book he was writing. Shortly after this, Linnaeus met a rich businessman named George Clifford. Clifford was a director of the

Dutch East India Company. He was a keen botanist and zoologist. The trading ships brought him many unusual plants and animals from abroad. His country estate was known throughout Holland for its wonderful botanic garden and its private zoo.

George Clifford was amazed by the way Linnaeus could classify plants that he had never seen before by opening up the flower and studying the stamens and pistils. Linnaeus was equally amazed by Clifford's wonderful garden. The hothouses were overflowing with tropical plants from India and other faraway places.

Linnaeus could think of nothing he wanted more than to spend all his time studying and describing the flowers in Clifford's garden. Clifford, who was often sick, liked the idea of having a live-in doctor. He asked Linnaeus to join his household. However, Burman did not want to lose his helper. The problem was solved when Burman admired a book in Clifford's library. "I happen to have two copies," Clifford said. "I will give you one if you will let me have

Linnaeus."[2] So Carl Linnaeus was traded for a rare book!

Linnaeus was as gifted at raising plants as he was at naming them. A banana tree that grew in one of the hothouses had never bloomed. Linnaeus repotted the plant in rich soil. He let the soil dry out and then soaked it, copying the pattern of tropical rainstorms. To everyone's

Linnaeus named the banana Musa paradisiaca *because he thought that it was the fruit of temptation in the Garden of Eden. This photo is from his bedroom in Hammarby, which is papered with pictures from a botany book.*

delight, the plant not only bloomed, but also produced fruit. Botanists came from all over Holland to see the miracle plant.

Earlier in the summer, Linnaeus had run into Peter Artedi, his old friend from Uppsala. They were both so busy that they did not meet again until September. Artedi was writing a book on the classification of fishes. The two young men spent a long time looking over Artedi's notes and discussing his ideas. It turned out to be the last time they met. A few days later, Artedi fell into a canal and was drowned. Linnaeus was terribly upset when he heard the tragic news. He kept the promise he had made back in Uppsala. He completed Artedi's book from his notes. It was published in 1738. Later, he named a plant in the parsley family *Artedia* in his friend's honor.

In the summer of 1736, Linnaeus visited England. He did not speak any English. In fact, he did not learn the language of any country he visited. He could always speak with educated people in Latin. Linnaeus made friends easily, but not all the botanists in England were ready to like him. He had turned the naming system of plants upside down. He had thrown out old names, replacing them with new ones to fit into his system. However, when other botanists met him, they were won over. They soon agreed that he had an amazing grasp of botany. It was almost impossible to show him a plant that he could not name.

When he returned to Holland, he threw himself into writing *Hortus Cliffortianus*, a book about the rare plants in Clifford's greenhouses. The description for each plant had to fit only that species. This was exacting work. It required research and detailed observations. Although Linnaeus worked long hours, he looked back on this period in Holland as the best time of his life. He was doing the work he loved, and Clifford treated him like a son.

In the fall of 1737, overwork caught up with Linnaeus. He became ill. He wanted to return to Sweden, but everyone begged him not to go. He agreed to stay on through the winter.

In early spring, Linnaeus received disturbing

news from Falun. One of his friends was courting Sara Lisa! It had not been hard for the friend to persuade Sara Lisa that Carl's true love was botany. Linnaeus had earned his degree in two weeks, but he had been gone for three years. Sara Lisa had reason to be tired of waiting.

Linnaeus began to make plans to return to Sweden, but he fell ill again. It was May before

Linnaeus returned from Holland with a medical degree, and a solid start on the many books that would make him famous.

he was well enough to travel. In spite of the time he had lost, he did not go straight home. He made a side trip to France. He spent a month visiting scientists in Paris.

Linnaeus's first stop in Sweden was Stenbrohult. Nils Linnaeus was proud to see copies of all the books that his son had published in the three years he had been gone. After spending two weeks with his father, Linnaeus set off for Falun. There he found Sara Lisa waiting for him.

Further Travels

DR. MORAEUS STILL HAD DOUBTS ABOUT his future son-in-law. He thought that Linnaeus needed a steady job with a good income before he married Sara Lisa. Moraeus had no idea how greatly foreign scientists respected the young botanist. No one in Sweden did. Linnaeus found it hard to come home and find that nobody cared "how many sleepless nights and weary hours"[1] he had spent on bringing order into the plant kingdom.

Linnaeus went off to Stockholm to set up a medical practice. Sara Lisa was again left behind in Falun. At first, Linnaeus was discouraged. He put up a sign, but no one came. He complained that "there was nobody who would even put a servant under my care."[2] Once again, he was concerned about money.

When Linnaeus most needed it, good fortune smiled on him. Though perhaps it is closer to the truth to say that he earned his good luck. One of his first patients was the wife of a senator. Linnaeus gave her a new kind of medicine that he had learned about in his recent visit to France. The medicine worked. The senator's wife told Queen Ulrika about Dr. Linnaeus. She went to see him, too. After treating the queen, the new doctor soon had all the patients he could handle.

Linnaeus got to know most of the important people in Stockholm. One of them was Count Carl Tessin. Tessin, a man of great influence, was interested in science. He arranged for Linnaeus to give lectures on plants. When the post of doctor to the Navy fell vacant, he suggested Linnaeus for the job. Linnaeus became the first president of the Stockholm Academy of

Sciences. This time, luck did play a role. The president was chosen from the membership by lottery.

Once again, Linnaeus was working very hard. Nowadays he would be called a workaholic. Within a year, he proved that he could support a wife in style. He and Sara Lisa Moraea were married in Falun in June 1739. After a month's vacation, Linnaeus returned to his busy life in Stockholm. Sara Lisa stayed behind with her parents. Carl and Sara Lisa paid a price for these long separations. They did not have a happy marriage.[3]

Linnaeus planted a botanical garden in Stockholm. In it, he grew plants that were useful in medicine. He led field trips to parks and out into the countryside. Although he was doing well as a doctor, in his heart Linnaeus was a botanist. His ambition was still to be Professor of Botany in Uppsala. He nearly got his wish in March 1740, when Olaf Rudbeck died. However, his old rival, Nils Rosén, was offered the job. Linnaeus was furious. He scoffed at the university's choice,

Carl Linnaeus was able to prove to Dr. Moraeus that he would be able to support Moraeus's daughter, Sara Lisa. Linnaeus's wedding portrait is shown here.

saying that Rosén "can't even recognize a nettle when he sees one."[4]

In January 1741, Sara Lisa Linnaea gave birth to a son. The baby was named Carl after his father. Sara Lisa was still staying with her parents in Falun. Linnaeus wrote to his wife telling her that he was overjoyed. He did not, however, go home to see his family right then.

Soon after this, the other professor of medicine at Uppsala retired. Linnaeus applied for his job. While Linnaeus was waiting to hear about it, he was given the chance to go on another adventure. Sweden was a poor country. Finding more natural resources would help the economy. The government asked Linnaeus to lead an expedition to the islands of Öland and Gotland. He was to look for minerals and to collect plants that could be used for medicines and for dye. He was also to look for clay soil that would be used to make fine pottery. This was exactly the sort of challenge that Linnaeus loved.

In May, just before he set out, Linnaeus learned that the job at Uppsala was his. He set

In January of 1741, Sara Lisa gave birth to a son, while in Falun, Sweden. Carl Linnaeus was busy at work in Stockholm at the time.

off, feeling that life was kind. On his way through Växjö, he stopped in to see his old teacher, Dr. Rothman. The doctor was proud that the student that no one else had believed in was now a famous scientist.

On reaching Öland in May, Linnaeus was delighted to find orchids growing wild. He had seen them in France, but had not expected to find them in Sweden. Today, people still travel to Öland to admire the orchids in the spring.

Linnaeus tramped all over the island, looking at everything. He was fascinated by rune stones from the Viking age. He found other reminders of the past. He was greatly impressed by the ancient ruins of Ismanstorpsborg. We still do not know who built the massive walls, or why. Linnaeus wrote, "In comparison to the other ruins . . . this was like a capital among hamlets. . . . There were rooms in all directions, but the plan could not be clearly discerned since the ruin was so overgrown with bushes and trees."[5]

Linnaeus kept telling his helpers to keep their eyes open. It was important to notice everything.

In May of 1741, Linnaeus went to explore the wildlife on Öland, an island off the coast of Sweden. Linnaeus was excited to find rune stones that date back to the days of the Vikings.

When some of the local people overheard him, they grew suspicious. At this time, Sweden was on the verge of war with Russia. The islanders thought that Linnaeus and his band of helpers were Russian spies. Linnaeus had to add a local man to his team to explain that they were only interested in the plants and rocks.

The band of naturalists moved on to Gotland, where Linnaeus was fascinated by the rich bird life. In his journal, he wrote about the razorbill, painting pictures with words: "With its black coat and white waistcoat, its wrinkled forehead and hooked nose and the effect it gives of wearing spectacles, it looks extremely comical when it walks. . . . If one passes below the cliffs and shouts loudly, 'Come on out!' or something like that, great quantities of birds fly out . . ."[6]

The group had trouble getting off Gotland. In his journal, Linnaeus wrote, "[T]here was no ship ready to sail and we were held there like prisoners. In the end we were obliged to make arrangements to risk our lives in the mail-boat which, like its skipper, was small, frail, ancient and unreliable. I don't know what happened but the man let us down and sailed without us."[7] Finally, they got back to Öland, and then to mainland Sweden.

Öland and Gotland Journey was published in 1741. It was the first book in which Linnaeus used binomial nomenclature all the way through. It was also the first book that he wrote in Swedish and not in Latin. The writing is colorful and easy to read. Linnaeus worried that a scientific book written in Swedish would not be read. He defended himself, saying that if people were allowed to write only in Latin, "the world would know less today than in fact it does."[8] He need not have worried. The book is still popular. Linnaeus's example and his writing still contribute to the Swedish people's love of nature today.[9]

Linnaeus and His Family

LINNAEUS GAVE HIS OPENING LECTURE at the University of Uppsala in October 1741. It was about the importance of exploring one's own country. He was now a happy man. He had reached his goal of becoming a professor. Sara Lisa, baby Carl, and he were at last living under the same roof. The only thing that kept his life from being perfect was that he had to teach anatomy and the other medical sciences. Nils Rosén taught all branches of natural history, including botany. The problem was easily solved. The two men switched jobs!

The Linnaeus family moved into Olaf

Rudbeck's old stone house, where Linnaeus had lived as a student while teaching Rudbeck's sons. It stood in the grounds of the university botanical gardens. The gardens had been badly neglected. Linnaeus set about putting them right. He wrote to friends in Holland and England asking for rare plants. He built new greenhouses and a tropical hothouse. Seven

When Linnaeus returned from Öland, he had a job waiting for him at Uppsala University. In October of 1741, he gave his opening lecture.

years later, the plant list ran to three thousand species.

Linnaeus collected unusual animals as well as plants. He was particularly fond of monkeys and parrots. One of his monkeys was a gift from Queen Ulrika. It had been a troublemaker in the palace, where it liked to steal silver buckles from the courtiers' shoes. His favorite parrot perched on his shoulder at mealtimes. If Linnaeus was late for lunch, the parrot would keep saying "Twelve o'clock, Mr. Carl!" until he appeared. It also called "Come in!" when it heard a knock at the door. Sometimes a visitor would then walk into the room and be puzzled to find no one there![1]

Linnaeus was a very popular teacher. He always lectured to overflow crowds. Students were attracted by his enthusiasm and his straightforward way of presenting new topics. He did not stick to natural history. He often lectured on nutrition, and even on child rearing. He said that children should eat often, but should only eat a little at a time. He disagreed

After his return to Uppsala, Linnaeus restored the university's botanical gardens, which had been neglected. Shown here is a picture of the University botanic gardens with the orangery. In the foreground is a house for one of Linnaeus's pet monkeys.

with the custom of tightly wrapping young infants. Babies should not be christened during cold weather or with cold water. He said that brown cows give the best milk. Not all of his ideas were good science. Some were based on the superstitions of his time.

On Saturdays, Linnaeus led large parties of students out into the countryside. Sometimes as many as a hundred and fifty people showed up. They all dressed alike in light, comfortable linen clothes. They carried butterfly nets and plant presses. These outings were similar to Linnaeus's earlier expeditions, but on a much bigger scale. He chose someone to take notes and someone to look after discipline. Someone was chosen to shoot birds. In those days, bird watchers carried a gun instead of binoculars. When a rare specimen was found, a student sounded a bugle. Everyone gathered around Linnaeus to learn about the specimen. At lunchtime, a table was set up with twenty places. The students who had made the most exciting finds got to dine with Linnaeus.

At the end of the day, they marched back into town waving banners, sounding horns, and beating drums. Linnaeus was in the lead. When they reached the botanic gardens, a cheer went up. "Long live science! Long live Linnaeus!" As you might guess, some of the less popular professors complained about the noise!

Meantime, the Linnaeus family was growing. In 1743, when little Carl was two, a sister, Lisa Stina, was born. A baby girl was born the following year, but she did not live. Then came Louisa in 1749 and Sara Stina in 1751. Another son, Johannes, was born in 1754 and died in 1757. Before the days of modern medicines, many young children died. The Linnaeuses' youngest child was born in 1757. Little Sophia would not have lived without her father's skill as a doctor. He described the birth in a letter to a friend: "Last Tuesday evening my wife bore me a daughter. She had a very difficult delivery and the girl was stillborn or died at birth, but nevertheless we blew air into her. . . . After quarter of an hour she began to breath a little. . . . Now she seems fairly well; but my wife is very weak, God help her!"[2]

Sophia thrived and grew up to be Linnaeus's favorite child. In spite of Linnaeus's lectures on child rearing, he was not always a good father, and his was not always a happy household.

Young Carl was taught at home. Linnaeus was determined that his son would follow in his footsteps. He did not seem to remember that he had chosen not to be clergyman like *his* own father, so Carl was taught a lot about botany. Most other subjects were neglected. Young Carl feared his parents more than he loved them. Even when he was a grown man, his mother still boxed his ears.

The girls, on the other hand, got no education at all. This was the way it was in those days. Linnaeus was actively against their being educated. They were not allowed to have French lessons. He wanted his daughters to grow up to be "hearty, strong housekeepers, not fashionable dolls."[3] Once, when Linnaeus was away, Sara Lisa Linnaea enrolled their youngest daughter in school. On returning home, Linnaeus soon put a stop to that idea.

Sara Lisa Linnaea herself was very strict with the children. Linnaeus sometimes sided with them against their mother, even when they deserved a scolding. One day, when Sophia tripped while carrying a tray of dishes upstairs,

Sophia was the youngest and favorite of Linnaeus's children. In later years she assisted her father in his work.

all the dishes broke. Sophia ran to her father. He told her not to be upset over such a little thing. He then bought a new set of dishes and claimed that he had smashed the other set because they were ugly.

During this period, Linnaeus published some of his most important work. Botanists agreed to accept the binomial names in *Species Plantarum* (1753) as the correct names, and to stop using names given before that time. The tenth edition of *Systema Naturae* (1758) became the starting point for binomial names for animals. Linnaeus was the first scientist to recognize that whales are mammals. In the tenth edition, he no longer used the name Quadrupedia ("four legs") for higher animals. Instead he called them Mammalia.

In 1758, Linnaeus bought a summer home, named Hammarby, about six miles from Uppsala. The whole family moved out there each spring as soon as the weather warmed up, and stayed until fall. They all loved Hammarby. Linnaeus built a square storeroom of stone on a rocky hill behind the house to keep his precious collections safe from fire. He called the room his museum.

Linnaeus used to attend the local church on Sunday mornings. His dog Pompe always went too. Linnaeus did not like to sit through long services. At the end of an hour, he would get up and walk out. When Linnaeus was sick, the little dog went to church by himself. Like his master, he always padded out after an hour!

Linnaeus's students followed him out to Hammarby. They lived in a nearby farmhouse. One of the students, Johan Fabricius, kept a journal. He painted a happy picture of his summers there with the Linnaeus family. On Sundays, everyone gathered at the farmhouse. They danced in the barn to the music of a violin. Sometimes Linnaeus watched from the sidelines. Other times he joined in, dancing with as much energy as his students. He liked to see young people enjoying themselves—the rowdier the better. Fabricius wrote, "I never shall forget those days, those hours, and it makes me happy whenever I recall them."[4]

The Linnaeus family were all early risers. Sara Lisa Linnaea saw to it that her daughters were out of bed by four o'clock on summer mornings. The girls took turns at the spinning

On Saturdays it was not unusual to find Linnaeus leading students on expeditions to look for rare forms of wildlife. Linnaeus kept his collection of plants at this museum in Hammarby.

wheel. Linnaeus was already working on his books. He joined his students for breakfast at six. Then he would talk about the orders of plants, sometimes going out into the countryside. Fabricius wrote, "Natural History was his whole life: he thought of nothing else."[5] That may explain why he was so set on his son Carl following in his footsteps.

The Apostles

AFTER LINNAEUS BECAME PROFESSOR AT Uppsala, he never lived outside Sweden again. His influence, however, reached far beyond Sweden's shores. Many of his students went overseas to look for plants in distant lands. The Linnaean system of naming allowed new plants to be fitted into the framework of known plants. This spurred scientists on to find new specimens.

The students who went off on these scientific expeditions became known as Linnaeus's "apostles." This is a good name for them. An apostle is a kind of missionary. As well as bringing back new plants, Linnaeus's students spread their teacher's fame throughout the world.

Looking for plants in foreign lands was dangerous work. Five of Linnaeus's students did not return. Christopher Tärnström, the first apostle, set off in 1746. He had a free passage to China on an East India Company trading ship. Linnaeus hoped he would bring back a tea plant, or at least some seeds. He also wanted some live goldfish. Tärnström, who was forty-three years old, was a pastor with a wife and children. He never reached China. He died of a tropical fever off the coast of Cambodia. His death was a terrible blow to Linnaeus.

Two years later, Peter Kalm set off for North America. First he went to Delaware, the home of many Swedish settlers. He then spent two and half years exploring Pennsylvania, New York, New Jersey, and Canada. Linnaeus was disappointed at how few letters he received from Kalm while he was gone. However, when the young explorer came home, he was soon forgiven. Linnaeus was sick at the time. On seeing all the pressed flowers and seeds that Kalm had brought back, Linnaeus claimed that "through joy at the plants, he no longer felt his illness."[1] In *Species Plantarum*, Linnaeus described seven hundred North American species. Ninety of them had been brought back by Kalm.

After hearing Linnaeus lecture on the plants of Egypt and Palestine, Fredrick Hasselquist made up his mind to see the plants in their native setting. Linnaeus tried to talk him out of going. Hasselquist was not a strong man. Linnaeus's worst fears came true. The young student died in Turkey "like a lamp whose oil is consumed."[2] He owed a huge amount of money at the time of his death. His collections and manuscripts could not be sent back to Sweden until the debt was cleared. Linnaeus appealed to the queen, who was very interested in natural history. She took care of the debt. Linnaeus was overwhelmed when he finally read Hasselquist's papers. He wrote, "God Bless the peerless Queen for letting me see them! . . . So admirable a travel journal has never before appeared. . . ."[3]

Peter Osbeck sailed for China in 1750 and returned safely two years later. He gave his whole collection to his professor. He also brought him a china tea set, decorated with his favorite flower, twinflower.

When the Spanish Ambassador asked Linnaeus who should study the plants in his

Often Linnaeus's students would visit foreign lands to collect specimens and spread the name of their teacher. One of his students, Peter Osbeck, returned from China with this teaset decorated with Linnaeus's favorite flower, twinflower.

country, Linnaeus suggested Peter Löfling. Löfling did such a good job that he was sent to South America to collect plants for "the Spanish Court, the King of France, the Queen of Sweden, and Linnaeus."[4] Linnaeus was happy to be included in such famous company.

Daniel Solander was a favorite student. Linnaeus hoped that Solander would marry his daughter Lisa Stina, but Solander went traveling instead. He sailed around the world with Captain Cook in 1768–71. This was the beginning of a tradition of including young naturalists on voyages of exploration. Sixty-three years later, Charles Darwin, the most famous naturalist-explorer, sailed around the world in the *Beagle*. Darwin was only twenty-one when he started out on his five-year voyage. His theory of evolution was based on observations made on the voyage.

After spending three years in South Africa, Carl Thunberg visited Japan. At that time, foreigners were not welcome in Japan. Thunberg collected plants in secret. He was so eager to learn more about Japanese plants that he went through pig and cattle food everyday looking for specimens to add to his herbarium. When he got to know some Japanese doctors, he taught them Linnaeus's system of classification. Like the other apostles, he was not afraid to put his life on the line while spreading the fame of his beloved teacher.

The Prince of Botanists

THE YEAR 1748 WAS NOT A GOOD ONE FOR Linnaeus. In May, he learned that his father had died. In his last words, Nils spoke of his son. "Carl is not here," he said. "Carl has brought me much happiness."[1]

Linnaeus was upset by his father's death. To make things worse, his career was not going well. Most of the problems were minor. The university was enforcing new rules. Professors needed permission to travel more than seven miles from Uppsala. Anyone who missed the beginning of term would lose pay. The most annoying rule was that professors would be fined for publishing books in another country. At any other time, Linnaeus would have taken this in his stride, but he felt that the publishing rule was directed at him. He was the only professor to whom it applied. When a friend complained about the way his botany students dressed and behaved on field trips, Linnaeus hardly slept for two months. He could understand some of the older and less successful professors' being jealous, but this was a trusted friend.

At this time, Linnaeus suffered periods of depression, but for long stretches, he enjoyed life as much as before. He still worked as hard as ever. Between 1749 and 1769, he wrote a hundred and seventy papers on everything from three-toed woodpeckers to the cause of epilepsy. His papers filled ten volumes. He also wrote several other books. In addition, he was busy with lectures, his students, and his family. He also found time to write letters to his many friends in Sweden and abroad.

Buying his country place at Hammarby had once again left Linnaeus short of money. He

As he grew older, Carl Linnaeus was awarded many honors. He was even knighted by the King of Sweden, which made him a nobleman.

recalled the pearl fishermen he had watched in Lapland. Would it be possible to make artificial pearls, he wondered. He had an idea of how it could be done. He decided to try it. He attached a tiny piece of limestone to a silver wire. Then he bored a hole in the shell of a mussel he had collected from the Fyris River. He inserted the limestone through the hole and fastened the wire to the shell. He put the mussel back in the river. Six years later, the rough limestone was completely covered. The mussel had made a large pearl.

At first, there was little interest in Linnaeus's experiment. Then, in 1762, Linnaeus was asked to bring his pearls to Stockholm. The government paid him two thousand dollars for his idea. In addition, he could choose his son or any other qualified person to be the next Professor of Botany at Uppsala.

Linnaeus was very happy. He could clear his debt and he could take care of young Carl's future. That same year, he was knighted by the king. As a nobleman, he became known as Carl von Linné. This is the name by which he is best known in Sweden, though he is still Carl Linnaeus to the rest of the world. That same year, the French Scientific Academy appointed him as a Fellow. He felt honored. The year 1762 was a very good one.

The following year was not so good. Linnaeus's health began to fail. Carl Jr. took over as Professor of Botany. He was a good botanist, but he had taken no examinations. He was not a popular teacher like his father. Linnaeus continued to lecture whenever he could.

In May 1764, Linnaeus had a serious fever. Dr. Rosén was called in. He treated and cured his old rival. The two men, who had always had so much in common, finally became friends. Two years later, when Rosén suffered a similar illness, Linnaeus looked after him.

In 1772, Linnaeus was still having health problems, but he could not bring himself to stop working. In a letter to a friend, he wrote,

You are right in saying that I ought not to work so hard. Latterly I have overtaxed my

brain, and now, on Monday next, I have to begin my lecture course. I tried for one term letting my son lecture; but I was like the old cart-horse whose legs grew stiff before it had been a month in the stall. . . .[2]

Linnaeus even took on the post of Rector of the University. The students respected him so much that during the six months he was rector, they caused him no trouble at all. In the past, they had been very wild. In his final address, given in Latin, Linnaeus spoke of the pleasure that came from studying natural history. The next morning, students called on him to thank him. They asked him to publish a Swedish translation of his speech.

After he suffered a stroke, Linnaeus had trouble with his memory. This was sad for someone whose memory for names had amazed the world. But there were still good days. He had many important visitors, including King Gustaf III. One wet day in August 1775, he arrived at Linnaeus's door. When he came into the house, the royal escorts were left sitting outdoors on their horses in the heavy rain. The king asked

After suffering a stroke, Linnaeus was forced to spend the majority of his time at home. Shown here is Linnaeus's country estate in Hammarby, Sweden.

Sara Lisa Linnaea if there was anything he could do for her. She asked him to let his escorts come inside, so that they could dry off and have something to eat. The king was surprised, but he agreed.

Carl Linnaeus died on January 10, 1778. He wanted to be buried in the church at Hammarby. That was not to be. He was buried in Uppsala

Cathedral. His funeral made a great impression on the mourners. One of them described the scene in these words:

> *It was a still and gloomy evening, the darkness relieved only by the torches and lanterns carried by the mourners, the silence broken only by the murmur of the large crowds lining the streets and heavy tolling of the great bell.*[3]

Linnaeus's library and all his collections were left to his widow and his children. Sir Joseph Banks, an Englishman, wanted to buy them. Carl Jr. refused. Carl moved them from Hammarby to Uppsala and took over their care. The collections were suffering from damp. Carl died late in 1783, less than six years after his father.

Sara Lisa Linnaea inherited the collection. She wrote to Sir Joseph in England, asking if he still wanted it. The news that it was for sale reached him while he was giving a breakfast party. He was no longer interested, but one of his guests was. James Edward Smith, a twenty-four-year-old medical student, bought Linnaeus's

After his death on January 10, 1778, Carl Linnaeus was buried at Uppsala Cathedral. Today, Linnaeus's specimen collection is stored at the headquarters of the Linnean Society of London, in Burlington House.

great collection and books for a thousand guineas. He got a bargain. The collection included 14,000 plants, 3,198 insects, 1,564 shells, about 3,000 letters, and 1,600 books.

The people of Sweden were furious when they learned that Linnaeus's collections were leaving the country. They have, however, been well cared for. Smith founded the Linnaean Society of London. The collections are still at the Society's headquarters in Burlington House. Scientists from all over the world travel there to see the famous manuscripts and original specimens. They treat the work of Carl Linnaeus, the Prince of Botanists, with admiration and respect.

Activities

Playing with Plants

According to Florence Cady's biography of Carl Linnaeus, when he was a child, "his toys were flowers."[1] We do not know what games Carl played with flowers. Here are two things to try with a potato:

To make a potato man, you need a potato and some grass seed. Cut a slice off the bottom of the potato so that it can stand. Now cut a slice off the top of the potato. Sprinkle grass seed on the cut surface. Keep the top of the potato moist.

After a few days, the grass seeds will begin to sprout. Your potato man now has a head of green hair. You might want to add eyes, a nose, and a mouth to your potato man. When his hair grows long, you can give him a haircut.

Here is a magic trick to try on your friends: Challenge them to make the water level drop in a glass bowl by adding a potato.

Here is how it is done: Cut one end off the potato and scoop out some flesh to make a small cup. Now stand the potato in the bowl of water. (You may have to shave off some potato to make it stand.) Put two spoonfuls of sugar in the hollow potato, adding a little water to make it dissolve.

A few hours later, you will find that most of the water in the bowl has disappeared. The hollow potato has filled up with water. You have just shown how plants take in water. Water moves through cell walls going from the weak solution to a stronger solution. This process is called osmosis.

Flowers for the Fourth of July

With the help of a little food coloring, you can turn a bouquet of plain white flowers red, white, and blue.

You will need:

- Several fresh white flowers, such as carnations

- Three small jars
- Red and blue food coloring
- A little cooking oil

Method:

1. Fill the jars with water.
2. Add a few drops of red food coloring to one jar and blue food coloring to another.
3. Put some flowers in each jar.
4. Pour a little oil onto the water. This helps to keep the water from evaporating.

After about two days, the flower should have taken up some of the colored water in the jar. To make a two-colored flower, split the flower stem. Now put one part in the red solution and the other part in the blue solution.

Making a Flower Press

Linnaeus kept track of all the flowers he found by making a herbarium. It is not hard to dry flowers. You can glue a dried flower on a card to make stationery. You can laminate it between plastic and make a bookmark as a gift.

You will need:

- Two sheets of Peg-Board about 8 x 12 inches (20 x 30 cm) or bigger
- Two straps that are long enough to go around the boards (old belts would do)
- Several sheets of blotting paper
- Old newspapers
- Fresh flowers

Method:

1. Lay the flowers between two sheets of blotting paper.
2. Put blotting paper between sheets of newspaper.
3. Cover with boards.
4. Bind the boards tightly with the straps.
5. Remove flowers after a few weeks.

A tennis racquet press can make a good flower press. You can also press flowers by laying them between sheets of blotting paper and placing a heavy pile of books on top. This method doesn't allow the flowers to dry, and they may not keep as well.

Making Your Own Indoor Garden

Linnaeus enjoyed making plants grow. People still visit his garden in Uppsala. He grew a wide range of plants in a small space. You don't need a lot of room for a garden. You can grow one in a glass jar.

You will need:

- A large glass jar with a lid
- Small pebbles or stones
- Potting soil
- Small plants, such as moss, ferns, and seedlings
- A spray bottle with water

Method:

1. Lay the jar on its side and put in a layer of stones.
2. Cover the stones with soil.
3. Plant your plants in the soil, pressing the soil down firmly.
4. Squirt enough water into the bottle to dampen the soil.
5. Put on the lid and place the jar where it is warm and light, but not in direct sunlight.

You can enjoy your jar garden without giving it much attention. The plants drink the water and release it into the air. The water then forms droplets that run back into the soil.

A Seed Collection

Flowering plants produce seeds, which make sure there's a next generation. Make a seed collection. You can look outdoors and find dandelion seeds. Pine cones have seeds in them. You can also collect seeds in your own kitchen or on your dinner plate. Corn on the cob is corn seeds. Beans are bean seeds. Look for seeds inside lemons, oranges, plums, cucumbers, avocados, and tomatoes.

Botany books often provide a key to help you find the name of a flower. Using a plant key is like going on a treasure hunt. You have to follow the clues. If you choose the right path, you learn the name of the flower.

Try making your own key to seeds you might find in your kitchen. Decide what characters to use to separate them. You could separate the seeds of avocado, plum, bean, corn, orange, lemon, tomato, and cucumber like this:

1. Seeds that are on their own.   Go to 2
   Seeds that like company.   Go to 3

2. Diameter bigger than a quarter: Avocado
   Diameter less than a quarter: Plum

3. Seeds that grew in a pod: Bean
   Seeds that were not in a pod.   Go to 4

4. Seeds in a fleshy or juicy fruit.   Go to 5
   Seeds sticking to a hard core: Corn

5. Fruit divided into segments: Orange
       Lemon
   Fruit not in segments: Tomato
       Cucumber

Once you have made a key, have a friend try it out to see how well it works.

The trees in the woods, the flowers in the fields, and the bugs in your garden have already been given names. Linnaeus and a lot of other scientists got there first. What if it were up to you? What would you name an oak tree? Or a dandelion? Or a firefly? What flower or bug would you name in honor of your best friend?

Some Examples of Binomial Nomenclature

Today, scientists still use Linnaeus's system of binomial nomenclature, but they have introduced some new groupings. The most common divisions are (from largest to smallest): Kingdom, Phylum, Class, Order, Genus, Species. Most scientists now recognize five Kingdoms: Animals, Plants, Fungi (mushrooms and funguses), Protists (microscopic living things), and Monerans (bacteria and blue green algae). Following are the scientific names (genus and species) of some familiar plants and animals.

   In this and all texts, a name followed by L. indicates a species named by Linnaeus. Sometimes names are changed to fit with new ideas. Linnaeus named the domestic cat *Felis Catus* (cat cat) but it is now *Felis domesticus*. Occasionally, Linnaeus's sense of humor comes through in his choice of names. He had a hard time separating very small creatures into distinct species. He settled on the name of *Chaos chaos* for a one-celled amoeba! Read the names below and think about why Linnaeus might have chosen these names.

Plants

COMMON NAME	SPECIES NAME	LITERAL MEANING
Banana	*Musa paradisiaca (L.)*	fruit of paradise
Broccoli	*Brassica oleracea (L.)*	cabbage, smelly
Buttercup	*Ranunculus acris (L.)*	little frog, bitter
Coneflower	*Rudbeckia occidentalis (L.)*	Rudbeck, western
Cucumber	*Cucumis sativus (L.)*	cucumber, cultivated
Daisy	*Chrysanthemum leucanthemum (L.)*	gold flower, white flower
Live oak	*Quercus virginiana (L.)*	oak, of Virginia
Marijuana	*Cannabis sativa (L.)*	hemp, cultivated
Orange	*Citrus sinensis (L.)*	citron, Chinese
Poison ivy	*Rhus toxicodendron (L.)*	sumac, poison leaves
Red clover	*Trifolium incarnata (L.)*	three leaves, blood red
Saguaro cactus	*Carnegiea gigantea*	Carnegie, giant
Sugar maple	*Acer saccharum (L.)*	maple, sugar
Tobacco	*Nicotiana tabacum (L.)*	Nicot's tobacco
Twinflower	*Linnea borealis (L.)*	Linnaeus, northern
Violet	*Viola sororia (L.)*	violet, of sister
White clover	*Trifolium repens (L.)*	three leaves, creeping
White pine	*Pinus strobus (L.)*	pine, pinecone

Animals

COMMON NAME	SPECIES NAME	LITERAL MEANING
Blue whale	*Balaenoptera musculus (L.)*	whale-wing, little mouse
Boa constrictor	*Boa constrictor*	snake, one that squeezes
Cat	*Felis domesticus*	cat, domestic
Dog	*Canis familiaris (L.)*	hound, domestic
Elephant (African)	*Loxodonta africana*	slanted tooth, African
Elephant (Indian)	*Elephas maximus (L.)*	elephant, great
Frog (American)	*Rana pipiens*	frog, chirping
Gray wolf	*Canis lupus (L.)*	hound, wolf
Harlequin duck	*Histrionicus histrionicus (L.)*	theatrical, theatrical
Honey bee	*Apis mellifera (L.)*	bee, honey-bearing
Horse	*Equus caballus (L.)*	horse, packhorse
House mouse	*Mus musculus (L.)*	mouse, little mouse
Human beings	*Homo sapiens (L.)*	human, wise
Mayfly	*Ameletus andersoni*	unstudied, Anderson's
Merganser duck	*Mergus merganser (L.)*	seagull, diving
Moose	*Alces alces (L.)*	elk, elk
Robin (American)	*Turdus migratorius (L.)*	thrush, wanderer
Salmon (Atlantic)	*Salmo salar (L.)*	salmon, salty
Toad (American)	*Bufo americanus*	toad, American
Tyrranosaurus rex*	*Tyrranosaurus rex*	tyrrant-lizard, king
Wild Turkey	*Meleagris gallopavo (L.)*	Meleager's (A Greek hero whose sisters were turned into birds),peacock

*extinct

Chronology

1707—Carl Linnaeus born in Råshult, May 23.

1717—Goes to school in Växjö.

1727—Enters University of Lund.

1728—Transfers to University of Uppsala.

1730—Gives botany lectures at Uppsala.

1732—Travels to Lapland.

1733—Death of Linnaeus's mother, Christina Linnaea.

1734—Leads expedition to Dalarna.

1735—Earns doctor's degree in Holland.

Systema Naturae is published.

Death of Peter Artedi.

1736—Journey to England.

1738—*Hortus Cliffortianus* is published.

Returns to Sweden from Holland.

Becomes a doctor in Stockholm.

1739—Marries Sara Lisa Moraea.

1741—Birth of son Carl.

Journey to Öland and Gotland.

Professor of Medicine at Uppsala University.

Öland and Gotland Journey is published.

1742—Professor of Botany.

1743—Birth of daughter Lisa Stina.

1748—Death of Linnaeus's father, Nils Linnaeus.

1749—Birth of daughter Louisa.

1751—Birth of daughter Sara Stina.

1753—*Species Plantarum* is published.

1754—Birth of son Johannes (died 1757).

1757—Birth of daughter Sophia.

1758   Buys Hammarby Estate.

1759—Tenth edition of *Systema Naturae* is published.

1762—Knighted by the King of Sweden.

1768—Twelfth edition of *Systema Naturae* is completed.

1772—Appointed Rector of the University.

1778—Dies in Uppsala, January 10.

Chapter Notes

Chapter 1

1. Wilfrid Blunt, *The Compleat Naturalist: A Life of Linnaeus* (London: Collins, 1971), p. 15.

2. Heinz Goerke, *Linnaeus* (New York: Charles Scribner's Sons, 1973), p. 95.

3. Surnames were not common in Sweden when Nils Linnaeus was a young man. When he started university, he needed a last name. He chose the name Linnaeus in honor of an ancient linden tree that grew on the family farm. Linnaeus is the masculine Latin form. Carl Linnaeus's mother's name is Christina Linnaea. Linnaea is the feminine form of the name Linnaeus.

4. Goerke, p. 89.

Chapter 2

1. Heinz Goerke, *Linnaeus* (New York: Charles Scribner's Sons, 1973), p. 13.

2. Wilfrid Blunt, *The Compleat Naturalist: A Life of Linnaeus* (London: Collins, 1971), pp. 17–18.

3. Goerke, p. 14.

4. Blunt, p. 18.

Chapter 4

1. Wilfrid Blunt, *The Compleat Naturalist: A Life of Linnaeus* (London: Collins, 1971), p. 30.

2. Ibid., p. 37.

3. Ibid., p. 38.

Chapter 5

1. Wilfrid Blunt, *The Compleat Naturalist: A Life of Linnaeus* (London: Collins, 1971), p. 41.

2. Ibid., p. 43.

3. Ibid., p. 51.

4. Ibid., p. 53.

5. Ibid., p. 55.

6. David Black, ed. *Carl Linnaeus Travels* (New York: Charles Scribner's Sons, 1979), p. 31.

7. Blunt, p. 60.

Chapter 6

1. Wilfrid Blunt, *The Compleat Naturalist: A Life of Linnaeus* (London: Collins, 1971), p. 77.

Chapter 7

1. Heinz Goerke, *Linnaeus* (New York: Charles Scribner's Sons, 1973), p. 96.

2. Wilfrid Blunt, *The Compleat Naturalist: A Life of Linnaeus* (London: Collins, 1971), p. 104.

Chapter 8

1. Wilfrid Blunt, *The Compleat Naturalist: A Life of Linnaeus* (London: Collins, 1971), p. 130.

2. Ibid.

3. Ibid., pp. 174–175.

4. Ibid., p. 135.

5. Carl Linnaeus, *Öland and Gotland Journey* 1741, translated from the Swedish edition of 1745 by Marie Asberg and William T. Stearn (London: Academic Press, 1973), pp. 78–79.

6. Blunt, p. 145.

7. Ibid., p. 146.

8. Ibid., p. 148.

9. Tore Frangsmyr, ed. *Linnaeus, the Man and His Work* (Los Angeles: University of California Press, 1983), p. vii.

Chapter 9

1. Wilfrid Blunt, *The Compleat Naturalist: A Life of Linnaeus* (London: Collins, 1971), p. 151.

2. Ibid., pp. 157–158.

3. Ibid., p. 176.

4. Ibid., p. 170.

5. Ibid.

Chapter 10

1. Heinz Goerke, *Linnaeus* (New York: Charles Scribner's Sons, 1973), p. 151.

2. Wilfrid Blunt, *The Compleat Naturalist: A Life of Linnaeus* (London: Collins, 1971), p. 185.

3. Ibid., p. 185.

4. Ibid., p. 188.

Chapter 11

1. Wilfrid Blunt, *The Compleat Naturalist: A Life of Linnaeus* (London: Collins, 1971), p. 194.

2. Ibid., pp. 228–229.

3. Ibid., p. 235.

Activities

1. Florence Cady, *Through the Fields with Linnaeus* (London: Longmans, Green, and Co., 1887), p. 20.

Glossary

binomial system of nomenclature—Two word way of naming.

dean—A high post in a cathedral or university.

genus (pl. genera)—The grouping of a species.

gibbet—Gallows.

herbarium—Collection of pressed and dried plants.

lichen—Type of plant that is made up of an alga and a fungus growing together.

mussel—Type of shellfish.

orangery—A greenhouse used especially for growing oranges in colder regions.

order—A major division in classification. Orders are divided into families, genera, and species.

pistil—The female part of a flower. It is made up of the stigma, style, and ovary.

pollination—The transfer of pollen from the anther to the stigma.

species—A group of organisms that closely resemble one another and are able to inter-breed.

stamen—Male part of a flower consisting of an anther and a filament. The head of the stamen, called the anther, bears the pollen.

taxonomy—The science of classification.

Further Reading

Forsthoefel, John. *Discovering Botany.* Buffalo, N.Y.: DOK Publishers, 1992.

Frangsmyr, Tore. Introduction by. *Linnaeus: The Man & His Work.* (rep. ed, rev ed.). Canton, MA: Watson Publishing International (Uppsala Studies in History of Science; Vol. 18), 1994.

Ganeri, Anita. *Plant Science.* Parsippany, N.J.: Silver Burdett Press, 1993.

Gotch, A.F. *Latin Names Explained: A Guide to the Scientific Classification of Reptiles, Birds and Mammals.* New York: Facts on File, 1995.

Hershey, David R. *Plant Biology Science Projects.* New York: John Wiley & Sons, Inc., 1995.

Margulis, Lynn. *Diversity of Life: The Five Kingdoms.* Springfield, N.J.: Enslow Publishers, Inc., 1992.

Mitchell, A. *The Young Naturalist.* Tulsa, OK: EDC Publishing, 1984.

Reynolds, J. *Far North.* San Diego, CA: Harcourt Brace & Company, 1992.

Zickgraf, Ralph. *Sweden.* Broomall, PA: Chelsea House Publishers, 1988.

Index